Mindfulness for Vegan Children

Written by Julia Barcalow, Ed.D & Illustrated by Kara Maria

For Lillyanna & Amelia, my inspiration
& for my Dad, for your unwavering love and support.

Mindfulness for Vegan Children

Text Copyright © 2020 by Julia Barcalow

Illustrations Copyright © 2020 by Kara Maria

Published by:
Vegan Kids Press, Sacramento, CA

www.vegankidspress.com

Typesetting by:
REBELCO

Printed in the USA

ISBN: 978-0-9980358-2-6

First Edition

Introduction

In a world brimming with distraction and over stimulation, it is important that children take time to quiet their minds and calm their emotions. Mindfulness is a practice that allows children to do just that. It teaches us how to be present, find our calm, and handle big emotions that can be hard to navigate. *Mindfulness for Vegan Children* incorporates a message of kindness and compassion for all animals and combines the five senses with a breathing practice to help children find their inner calm and connect with nature. It also includes a Mindfulness Mantra for Vegan Children that can be used as a positive affirmation throughout daily life. I hope you enjoy this book with your family as much as I have enjoyed it with mine.

Breathe in love.

Breathe out light.

There are animals everywhere who need us to show them that we care.

They inhabit the sea,

land,

and sky.

I watch them swim,
          run, and fly.

I am them, and they are me,
and we are all part of earth's family.

Let's be mindful of the way
we spend each and every day.

I watch as the dolphins swim in the sea,
and **taste** the salty water that splashes on me.

Breathe in and see the dolphins swim.
Breathe out and taste the salty water.

I soar with the birds way up in the sky.
I **feel** the air on my face as the wind blows by.

Breathe in and soar with the birds.
Breathe out and feel the wind.

I sit in the garden with the butterflies and bees, and **see** sunflowers growing as tall as the trees.

Breathe in and see the butterflies and bees.

Breathe out and see the sunflowers.

I walk through the forest
with the rabbits and bear,
and breathe in the **smell**
of the crisp, clean air.

Breathe in and walk
with the rabbits
and bear.

Breathe out and smell
the crisp, clean air.

I stand in the pasture with a cow and her calf.

The **sound** of their chewing makes me smile and laugh.

Breathe in and see the cow and her calf.

Breathe out and hear them chew the grass.

I explore the mountains

where the **giant** pandas eat bamboo.

I stop to take a **drink** of
the early morning dew.

Breathe in and see the pandas eat bamboo.
Breathe out and taste the morning dew.

I run through the fields with horses all around. I feel the power of their hooves beat against the ground.

Breathe in and run
with the horses.

Breathe out and feel their
hooves beat against the ground.

I climb with the monkeys up high in the tree, and gaze at the world that is all around me.

Breathe in and climb with the monkeys. Breathe out and see the world all around.

I lie by the lake while the fish swim around.

I **smell** the sweet flowers that cover the ground.

Breathe in and see the fish in the lake.
Breathe out and smell the flowers.

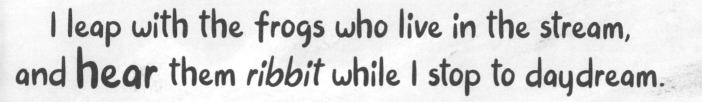

I leap with the frogs who live in the stream,
and **hear** them *ribbit* while I stop to daydream.

Breathe in and leap
with the frogs.

Breathe out
and hear them *ribbit*.

I dance through the meadow as day turns to night.

I marvel at every touch, taste, sound and sight.

Breathe in and **see** the meadow. Breathe out and **feel** the soft grass between your toes.

Breathe in and **smell** the colorful flowers. Breathe out and **hear** the birds sing.

Breathe in and **taste** the juicy blueberries. Breathe out and **see** the animals graze.

I think of animals, **large** and small.

I am thankful for them all.

They need our love. They need our light.
They need us to protect their rights

Breathe in love.

Breathe out light.

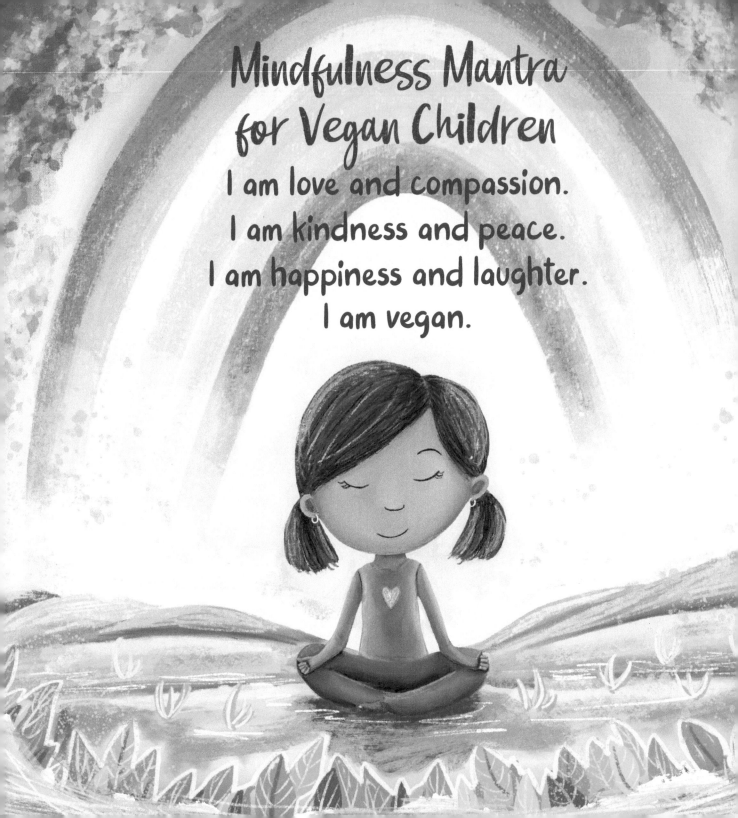

Mindfulness Mantra for Vegan Children

I am love and compassion.
I am kindness and peace.
I am happiness and laughter.
I am vegan.

CPSIA information can be obtained
at www.ICGtesting.com
Printed in the USA
LVHW070150021120
670424LV00019B/569

* 9 7 8 0 9 9 9 8 0 3 5 8 2 6 *